Praise for A Flower in the Desert

A FLOWER IN THE DESERT IS AN ILLUMINATING TEACHING ON awareness and selflessness, following in the provocative and creative tradition of Zen Master Bankei, Wei Wu Wei, and Douglas Harding. David Lang's prose is spare and elegant—the book is a delight to read.

Joseph Goldstein, author of *Insight Meditation*

THIS BOOK IS THE ADVENTURE OF EMPTINESS, CONTEMPLATIVE and unassuming. It is a journey into the unknown space surrounding us all. It opens the reader up to the infinite possibilities in the moment at hand, no matter where we are, or what we may have.

Sharon Salzberg, author of *Lovingkindness: The Revolutionary Art of Happiness*

DAVID LANG HAS WRITTEN AN EERILY ORIGINAL AND POETIC account of his spiritual epiphany. This book will behead you, and you'll be thankful for the favor.

Wes Nisker, author of *Crazy Wisdom*

LIKE A FLOWER IN THE ARID DESERT OF TODAY'S MATERIALISTIC and mentalistic culture, David Lang helps us to turn the spotlight, the consciousness searchlight, inwards—meaning, more deeply—and to find out who and what we are, how we fit in to the bigger picture, and fulfill the meaning of our lives.

Lama Surya Das, author of *Buddha Is as Buddha Does*

THIS BOOK IS AT ONCE POETRY AND MEDITATION ON A JOURNEY of discovery that unfolds, moment by moment, literally right before our noses.... I believe this book makes a unique and valuable contribution to authentic inquiry, and the simple beauty of its language enhances its power and accessibility.

> Dr. Kaisa Puhakka, former editor of *The Journal of Transpersonal Psychology* and professor of psychology at the California Institute of Integral Studies

DAVID LANG'S A FLOWER IN THE DESERT SPEAKS TO US IN exquisitely simple language about deeply complex questions: Who am I? What guides me? Where am I going?—only to discover that in "nothing" lies "everything." We can learn to be the flower in the desert by letting this spare and humble story draw us quietly into our inner blossoming.

> Gabriele Rico, author of *Writing the Natural Way*

A Flower in the Desert

Images from the Headless Way

DAVID LANG

NON-DUALITY PRESS

A FLOWER IN THE DESERT
First edition published August 2012 by NON-DUALITY PRESS

© David Lang 2012
© Non-Duality Press 2012

Author photo by Simone Anne Lang

NON-DUALITY PRESS | PO Box 2228 | Salisbury | SP2 2GZ
United Kingdom

ISBN: 978-1-908664-25-9
www.non-dualitypress.org

To Carol and Simone, whose love
I will always treasure

And to Douglas, who showed me the Desert

The Key of the Kingdom

This is the key of the kingdom:
In that kingdom is a city,
In that city is a town,
In that town there is a street,
In that street there winds a lane,
In that lane there is a yard,
In that yard there is a house,
In that house there waits a room,
In that room an empty bed,
And on that bed a basket -
A basket of sweet flowers:
Of flowers, of flowers,
A basket of sweet flowers.

Flowers in a basket,
Basket on the bed,
Bed in the chamber,
Chamber in the house,
House in the weedy yard,
Yard in the winding lane,
Lane in the broad street,
Street in the high town,
Town in the city,
City in the kingdom—
This is the key of the kingdom,
Of the kingdom this is the key.

Anonymous

Contents

Introduction

In 1970, when I was 17, my life was turned upside down by a very simple thing: a pointing finger—my pointing finger.

I was in an ordinary room with ordinary-looking people, but my finger was pointing at what was extraordinary—indeed (it seemed) impossible: a place where there were no things, no people, no colors, no shapes, no movement—in fact, where there was nothing at all.

My finger was pointing at me.

I was not at all prepared for this vision of nothingness. Raised in a conventional English family and educated in a conventional English school, where things out of the ordinary, no matter how far out of the ordinary, were still *things*, I expected to see things everywhere I looked. But there in that room, following the directions of the workshop leader, the philosopher and mystic Douglas Harding, I was instead looking directly and unequivocally at nothing.

Or, to be more precise, at no-thing, for what I saw turned out to be not just nothing. It was, for a start, awake, had always been awake, and would always be awake. Which was absurd, for that meant that I had always been awake—long before I was born—and that I would always be awake—long after I was dead.

In one brief experience, the basic assumptions of my life had come undone, and I began a new life based on the astonishing experience of being made of no-thing.

Here is the story of that life—an ordinary life lived in the light of the extraordinary.

I

A Path

Path 1

I am lying in bed, slowly waking. I don't know the time, but I can tell by the two pale rectangles of light glimmering in the darkness that dawn is near. In the distance, I hear the sound of a train.

Distance? An assumption. The rolling, rumbling sound, small and faint, vibrates in the silence of this room.

Lying in bed? A convenient lie. For in the darkness, among these warm and comfortable sensations, no bed or body appears. Beyond these thoughts, no mind governs.

I reach out my hand, searching for my watch on the floor. By its battery light, I see it is six o'clock. I have an hour before my family wakes—time to write these words.

At this moment, three paths are crossing. Three? Yes, three. For besides your path, which beyond the pages of this book forks into your past and future, unknown to me, and besides my path, selected bits of which glimmer in the darkness between the pages ahead, there is a third, broad path upon which we can travel together. It stretches from this book in front of you to You and from my computer screen in front of me to Me. Not such a long path, eh? And not particularly

interesting, either, you might think. But—forgive me—
you would be wrong. For here is a path showered with
more magic than the most fantastic fairytale. Step onto
this one-foot-long path, and you can walk all the way
to infinity. Pass through this mild countryside, and you
will encounter such dangers as will challenge you to
risk, and lose, your life. Arrive, both dead and alive,
at your destination, and you will find that your end is
your beginning, and that you have never left, since even
before you were born, this marvelous home.

What end? What beginning?

The answers fork into paradox and vanish below
the horizon of words.

"But look," I say, "over here. How clear the sky! How
beautiful the view!"

But I am getting ahead of myself. Come. Let us go
together. The door is open.

Path 2

When I was seventeen—I'm going back almost thirty years now—my own path brought me to a featureless, unpromising place.

I had prayed to God ever since I was a child, committing myself each day to serving God, asking for God's help. But at seventeen, walking out of the church one day and looking up at the grey clouds hanging in stillness over the slate rooftops of my town, I realized that, despite all my dedication and desire, I didn't know whether God existed or not. I had spoken to God, but God hadn't spoken to me. Was God there, beyond the silence and the apparent indifference? I didn't know. And I concluded on that day that I would never know.

For after all, who was I? An unremarkable schoolboy on the edge of adulthood. If the great minds of history hadn't been able to prove God's existence, I wasn't going to do any better. The arguments seemed to be no more than arguments: debatable, inconclusive, joining together in the end in the age-old appeal to faith, like various streams flowing downhill to the one great river of hope. The faith that the vicar had preached from his well-built, wooden pulpit could easily be—at best, perhaps—nothing more than a sincere wish. At worst—well, opiate for the masses. How could I tell?

I couldn't. The clouds said nothing. The rooftops said nothing. And the people in the streets of the market town, their faces ruddy from breathing the cold, winter air, went about their business, laughing at each other's stories, making arrangements for deliveries, driving off home. Was God here in the town, or outside the town, or anywhere? Screwing up the unanswerable question and throwing it in a litterbin, I walked away.

Path 3

"What are you going to be when you grow up?" The question made me cringe inside. How, after walking through cornfields on a summer's afternoon, clouds shaped like great dollops of cream drifting across the far, blue sky, butterflies dancing with abandon in the still infinitude of the sun, how could I even imagine I would grow up into anything so limited as a person, let alone a person defined by the path of a career?

For to be someone meant that I would be reduced from the All into a piece of the All. I would be confined within the edges of a thing, like a great polar bear pacing back and forth, back and forth, in a small cage at the zoo, its freedom reduced to a slobbering memory. I would be trapped for ever inside the hell of an object called *me*.

Of course, the people who asked me this question, many of whom were inside my head, weren't asking a metaphysical question. They simply wanted to know what job I was going to choose to pay my way in the world. Was I interested in being a teacher? Would I be an engineer like my father? (Was I going into the family business?)

But I was no longer a child. At seventeen, it is true, I could delay the decision a little longer by going to university and immersing myself in novels and poetry, which I did. And I could take some time to identify with one of my heroes, Jack Kerouac, that free spirit of the road, and travel overland to India, which I did. But I had also seen the hobos. I did not want to pursue my freedom the rest of my days sitting on a park bench drinking cheap wine.

And so before me I found the beginning of a path and the decision that was not a decision but an imperative: to take, today or tomorrow or the next day, but inevitably to take, that step which led away from freedom and, of course, there it was in the end, toward death.

Path 4

I walk, at sixteen, out of my home in England, taking the footpath along the side of the house towards the fields. It is an old path, the black, drystone walls on either side of it bulging as if, over time, they have become pregnant. As I walk, my attention is split. I look down at the large roots crisscrossing the floor of the path like the veins on my grandfather's hand, and I lift my feet carefully so as not to trip. But I want to look up, too. For above me is an enticing, overarching lacework of branches, cascading with a myriad pointed, red-brown leaves. I know these trees well. Here on the left is one whose trunk forks, becoming two trees in one, and inside the fork is hidden, away from the path, a dark hole. An owl's home, perhaps.

The path inclines slightly up a hill, at the top shedding its walls and surrounding trees and entering an open field. I love this place. At night I come here, feeling my way through the narrow darkness of the tree-lined path until, like a baby at birth, I issue forth into the wide arms of the field and the light of the stars. I lie down on the belly of the Earth, my eyes searching the sky for the patterns of the constellations, for the red gem of Betelgeuse, for the huddle of the Pleiades. I am at home in the stars.

But in the daytime, today, the path does not stop here. It skirts the field along two sides, exits through a gate beside a lone, stone-built house, and crossing a road to pass through another field, finds itself at the edge of a valley. I stand at this edge, enjoying the view. Below me, the fields fall away steeply. Green hedges, homes to sparrows, rim the fields. What is down there, where the path is lost in the folds of the valley? A stream? Yes. And beyond that? The evening meal with my mother and father, brother and sister. And further into the distance, a myriad images cascading down twenty-eight years and opening now into this sunny, winter day in California.

Does the path stop here in the present? I don't know. I glance ahead from the edge of the moment and see more images, some frightening, some enticing. But there is no certainty. I don't even know if, in this earthquake-prone state, I will live beyond today. Will I reach old age, as I hope? Will I be happy or sad, rich or poor, alone or surrounded by family and friends? And even if I do live till I'm ninety-nine, what then? Will the path end there on that sad height, or will I lie again in the womb of the earth and then ride a star-lit path into another world?

I do not know and may never know. The journey could end at any time in ambush and oblivion. And my ignorance arises not only from looking into the future. When I look back along the way that I have come, beyond that walk across the English fields, back down the years till the images become sparse—my uncle swinging me around his body so wildly, the smoke rising from the gardener's leaf pile behind the nursery school, the large, black spider sitting in perfect stillness at the center of its dewdrop web—when I look back as far as I can see, I find there also that I know nothing. Beyond those memories is an edgeless absence of experience where all I can say is that I have no memories. I am surrounded by questions. Where did I come from? Where am I going? Why does my path seem to peter out at its beginning as it does, from my present view point, at the end? Was my beginning an awakening from an oblivion occasioned by an ambush of which I have no recollection?

But there is another question, one which underlies these questions about the beginning and ending of my path of images and memories. Who, naked of those images and memories, began this journey, got dressed in this person, and then, having crawled and walked and run along this path, will surely stumble and fall and, naked once again, exit without trace? Who is that one? Who, before and beneath and after all experiences, am I? And who, underneath your experiences, holding this book in your hands, travelling your path, are you?

Path 5

At the age of nine, I went to a boys' boarding school in the country. Behind the school, beyond the farm and the road, was the moor, a treeless expanse of heather and rocks that stretched for miles. On clear days, climbing up from the road through the bracken and reaching the plateau of the moor, I could follow the narrow, winding sheep trails until the views of the valley and the school had sunk far below the horizon. Up there, I was left with only the wind and the high, hovering notes of the larks for company. What a luxury it was to leave the crammed quarters of the school on a Sunday morning and, choosing my own direction across the moor, let my mind sink deep into its vast aloneness and the vastness and aloneness of the sky.

Once or twice a week in the winter, after lunch, most of the boys in the school had to do a run called 'Short Johnny on the Moor.' It led up onto and then along the edge of the moor for a mile or two before descending steeply to cross a stream and head back to the school. Short Johnny was really an easy run, though cold rain made it hard.

More extended runs were for senior boys only. 'Long Johnny on the Moor' started and finished in about the same places on the moor as its shorter version, but it stretched out in the middle for an extra mile across the rolling hillocks of bracken. And then there was the 'Ghost House,' a run which headed straight up onto the moor and, crossing the remains of a Roman road, made a long loop around a disused game-shooters' shelter that stood alone among the sheep and the changeable weather.

However, there was another run, an almost legendary run, which happened just once every year or so. This run, called 'Dick Hudson's,' was for volunteers only, boys who wanted to see if they could endure a long run. For it was very long, passing the Ghost House in its early stages and reaching far across the moor to a place beyond any landmarks I knew.

In my last year at the school, when I was twelve, I set out on the Dick Hudson run with a teacher and four other boys, three of whom had run it before. We began on the familiar track past the farm to the gate at the road above the school. How tiring the first part of a run always was for me before I got used to the repetitive rhythm of my feet reaching, one after the other, for the ground ahead and pulling it under me. My chest ached. The energy in my legs felt heavy and old. At the gate, I paused to rest and looked up at the moor, canopied by grey clouds. The other runners passed through the gate, and after closing it, I began again, pushing my body across the road and climbing the steep hill to the sheep trails and the open moor above.

When we reached the moor, the clouds had descended to the ground and had formed a mist there. We headed into it together, aiming in the direction of the Ghost House. As we ran, my body became used to the effort of running. The ache in my chest melted away. The tiredness evaporated. I breathed deeply the cool, damp air and became absorbed in the group's movement across the moor.

In half an hour, the Ghost House appeared through the mist. I glanced at its glistening stone walls and iron roof. Here many times before, I had swung around the building and headed back toward the school, like a comet at the furthest edge of its orbit responding to the distant pull of the sun. But this time we did not turn back. We kept moving forward into what was for me unfamiliar moor.

I was running near the back of the group. One boy was behind me, puffing heavily. In front of me was the teacher. Ahead of him were the three other boys, the ones who had, a year or two previously, done this same run. They were full of energy, searching together for the way they had come before, competing for the firmest sense of direction, running ahead as the leaders of the group. Gradually, they got further in front until they had become a separate group, running out there on the edge of my consciousness.

Time stretched, measured only by the constant rhythm of my feet pounding the ground and my lungs inhaling the cool air. The heather and rocks flowed by. I was a boat, ploughing through waves on my way into the unknown, the grey mist a veil that lifted only to reveal another veil beyond it. I ran, following the path, the teacher, the others, drawn on by the impetus of the group, my mind submerged in the physicality of the run.

"I can't go on!" The sudden words came from the boy behind. I stopped and turned, surprised. He was standing on the path, his face, arms, and legs flushed.

"All right, Tim." It was the teacher speaking. He also had stopped and was walking past me to stand in front of the boy. "Do you think you can find your way back on your own?" The boy nodded. The teacher looked around into the mist and then back at the boy. "OK. We'll see you at the school." I watched for a moment as the boy turned and began walking back. He was soon gone. The teacher and I turned again and resumed running.

But the run was different now. In those few moments with Tim, we had lost touch with the other boys. As I looked ahead, all I saw was thickening mist and sheep trails branching left and right, petering out in the greyness. I couldn't sense the other boys. They were somewhere ahead, but their shapes had dissolved in the mist. They were gone.

The teacher quickened his pace. I followed, pushing my energy to keep up with him, grasping harder at the ground to move it faster beneath me. But I couldn't do it. I didn't have the reserves for extra effort. Soon the teacher too was disappearing into the mist ahead of me.

He looked back and stopped. "I need to catch the other three," he said quickly. "You go back to the school, OK?" Then he left me.

I stood there for a moment, facing the mist and the empty moor, a dismal view of heather and rocks fading into emptiness. I was alone, tired, in a place I didn't know.

I turned and ran back along the path. In a few minutes the path branched, one sheep trail carelessly meandering off to the left, another meandering off to the right. Unsure, I stopped. I hadn't seen this fork before.

15

The two paths looked the same. I glanced around, afraid. Stories told in my dormitory's darkness rose to mind—sucking bogs, bottomless holes, search parties returning empty-handed. I wished I were there, scared in my bed. A wind ruffled my shirt. Anxiety seeped into my heart, welled up into my throat and eyes.

· ·

I stand at the window of the apartment, looking at the rain falling on the alley and the dilapidated fence and on the church and apartment buildings beyond the fence. Through a gap between the buildings, I see cars swishing back and forth along Guerrero Street. I am depressed. At thirty, I have no career. Twice a week I take my high-end degree and my heavy heart to the houses I clean. Three times a week, if there is work, I take them to lift rocks and clear briars for a gardening company. But today the rain has cancelled the gardening, and I am fed up with reading and dreaming and waiting and hoping. Yet I am afraid to move. Afraid to make a phone call, afraid to put on my polyester suit, afraid to tell the interviewing eyes how good I am at what I imagine I can do. I can't imagine I can do anything anymore. Before me, as the rain falls, Guerrero Street turns into a shadowy, alien river.

· ·

I chose one of the paths and began running. When the path branched again, I chose again, and ran on, surrounded by mist. Nothing was familiar. The sheep trails were a complicated spider's web and I a desperate fly. I ran across bracken and rocks and paths. I ran, not knowing, afraid, trying to conjure the lights of the school out of the mist like a second-rate stage magician. But all I saw, in front, to the sides, behind, were the moor and the mist.

I ran on and on until at last the flatness of the moor gave way to an edge. The trail I was on descended, taking me down through bracken and fading light to a stream. Here, suddenly, as if it had never been, the mist lifted, and I could see beyond the stream a broad, gravel-and-clay track. I crossed the stream and stood on the track, looking around me like a sleepwalker slowly waking. For I knew where I was—nowhere near where I should have been, but that didn't matter. I was no longer lost. I was instead standing on a track that, like a friend, extended a hand to me and with its other pointed out the familiar road below. Beyond the road, I knew I would find the old farm track that led across the fields back to the school.

Something at my feet caught my eye. Lying on the gravel was a small, wooden doll's head, the size of a marble. I picked it up, turning it in my fingers. Two black dots in the red face eyed me. A curved line smiled at me.

I held the head tightly in my hand like an amulet and ran down the track to the road.

Path 6

I would be arrogant and stupid to think that my path
has to be your path, or that the path I am on is *the* path,
though I used to think that way. How could it be? Have
you been lost on Ilkley Moor? Have you been swung by
my uncle around and around in dizzy ecstasy? Have you
been imprinted with an image of the full moon rising
over the edge of a lake in the mountains of California?

"But," a voice inside my head objects, "you said at
the beginning there was a third path which we could
travel together. What happened to that?"

"Nothing happened to that," another voice replies.
"But you must forget about paths. The important thing
is to find, not seek. Traveling on a path for its own sake
becomes in the end wandering."

"Look, you two," a third voice counters, "there is
a path, and there isn't a path. It's everyone's path, and
it's your path and my path, and it's no-one's path. And
when you reach the end of it, you are at the beginning
you never left. It's mystery and paradox. Stop trying to
figure it all out."

Well, OK. There is some truth in each of these posi-
tions. But all this talk seems rather complicated. I meant
something quite simple and concrete when I referred to
a third path, too simple and concrete, perhaps. I don't

18

know whose the third path is, or whether it really is a third path, or if it's *the* path or just *a* path. All that seems rather silly now. But I do know where it is, and I know where it goes, just as I know the same things about the path I used to take across the fields near my home when I was a kid. In a way, it's the same kind of path. But no more talk. Let me show it to you, just as my friend, Douglas, showed me twenty-eight years ago.

Path 7

We are sitting in a circle with eight people in a small, oak-paneled room. Glancing to the end of the room, you see tall, narrow windows with lead-rimmed panes, befitting this large, old, country house outside London. Beyond the windows are trees, dark with leaves, standing against a backdrop of blue sky and drifting white clouds. A woodpigeon's cooing, soft like a flute's song, weaves in through the open window.

The workshop has already begun. You turn back and focus on the speaker seated opposite, a sixty-year-old man with white hair and clipped white beard— Douglas Harding, apparently. What is he saying—that he has no head? I exchange glances with you. What have we got ourselves into?

"But it's no use my *talking* about it," Harding says. "I could go on and on talking about it till I was blue in the face, and it wouldn't make a bit of difference to whether or not you got it." He seems both relaxed and animated. "You have to *see* it, not just listen to me talk *about* it. And," he adds, "I have a little experiment that will make it impossible for you *not* to see it."

To Harding's right, a middle-aged woman with glasses is smiling broadly. Next to her is a wiry, younger man—late twenties, I guess (though at seventeen, late twenties seems already middle-aged)—sitting with knees close together and shoulders hunched at an angle away from Harding. On Harding's other side is a middle-aged man, his head almost bald and his nose and chin slightly hooked. The man is smiling, too. The woman next to him, I am guessing, is his wife, a pale-faced woman carrying a soft, distant look in her eyes.

"Lift up your forefinger," Harding says, "and point it at the ceiling." He points his resolutely up, and eight other hands, including mine, point at the ceiling like a sea anemone waving its soft spines in the ocean currents. "You have actually to do this," he says, looking around the circle. "You will get nothing, absolutely nothing out of this experiment if you don't do it." His voice has become stern. The hunched-up man raises his hand and points at the ceiling.

"Please look at what you are pointing at," Harding says, "a white plaster ceiling with cracks running across it. Now look at what you are pointing with—your finger. Would you notice, please, that both the ceiling and your finger are things? That is, both have edges. Both have color. Both have texture. They are in a symmetrical relationship with each other, one thing pointing at another thing."

OK.

"Now bring your finger down from the ceiling and point at someone across the circle from where you're sitting. Point at his or her head. What do you see? A hairy, eight-inch meatball sitting on a pair of shoulders? Aren't your finger and that meatball in the same kind of relationship that your finger and the ceiling were in before—thing pointing at thing?"

On the end of my finger I balance the smiling woman's head. Meatball?

"Now bring your finger down yet again, pointing it at your foot. Surely it's the same situation again, a thing pointing at a thing."

It is. I glance at you. You roll your eyes, amused.

"Turn your finger around now and point it at your tummy. Finger to tummy? Thing to thing, isn't it?"

Yes.

"Point your finger at your chest. Isn't it finger to chest?"

It is.

"Now point your finger at your face. What do you see? Don't look at me. Look at what your finger is pointing at. Is it pointing at a face? Is your finger, which is a thing, pointing at another thing which is colored and edged and textured and shaped, which is in symmetry with your finger? Or isn't it pointing at a no-face, a no-thing, an emptiness, a clarity which goes on and on for ever and ever, as clear as glass?"

I stare at this clarity. It is indisputable—so clear, like glass, like water, like light. How have I missed this? Right here. Unbelievable: I am made of air and nothingness.

I look over at you, and your face shines in the emptiness. We are at the beginning—and the end—of a journey, a path new and striking and yet leading to, not away from, ourselves, leaping wildly from the tips of our pointing fingers into you, into me, into this openness here, our first and last and deathless destination.

II

The Desert

Desert 1

It is as if I am walking up the main street of my town, not thinking much about anything, perhaps with a list in my head of what I ought to do to get my life on track, or of what I need to buy at the supermarket, the wind blowing cold in my face, so that I draw the lapels of my coat more tightly around my neck and step more resolutely on the pavement as it inclines toward the church at the top of the hill, and there by the café on the left, turning the corner, as I have turned it before, into that little lane between the old stone buildings, I walk into a vast and sandy desert.

I turn around, looking at where I have come from, and there is the familiar main street framed by the edges of the lane. A shopper appears out of the edge of the building on the right, struggling up the hill, holding her hat against the strengthening wind. Then she's gone, into the edge of the building on the left, as if she had never been. A car zooms out of the edge of the building on the left, a blue blur of a stationwagon heading down the street, and disappears just as suddenly into the edge of the building on the right, the edge from which the woman emerged.

These edges. They are like magicians' hats. What will jump out next?

I turn back. The desert! In my town! How am I going to explain this?

Desert 2

When I look here at this no-face, I see an absence. The absence of my eyes and my cheeks, my mouth and my chin, my teeth. The absence of my skin. The absence of my structure, of my skull, and of the brain inside my skull. The absence of my edges. The breath that moves like a gentle breeze, rising and falling, rising and falling, moves not between my edges, those imagined hollows bounded by cartilage and bone. It moves rather in openness, a wind blowing across a vast desert where nothing is. It moves in and out, in and out, of absence.

I examine this absence closely, but I can find nothing. My heart flips. Nothing! Nothing at all! Is this my substance, then? Is this what I am made of?

I am like a traveler who foolishly has entered a vast and forbidding desert and has vanished without trace. I have not simply lost my way. I have lost my self. Not even a bleached bone remains. Only the wind, rising and falling, rising and falling, is heard.

Desert 3

This desert is so empty. It is the emptiest place I have ever seen. No mountains skirt it with edges where my eyes can alight. No rocks, no dunes challenge my feet. No plants grow here. Nothing moves, not even a sand grain stirred by the wind.

And yet the desert is beautiful, so full of light. Light like the clearest spring water. Light like new glass. Light like mountain air, in which each detail of the valley below—the copse, the sinewy river, the houses dotted along the road—appears preternaturally close, like a miniature landscape. The light shines everywhere. No place, not even the darkest place, is without the light.

I walk down the steep path into the valley, cairns like buttons guiding my way. Here the houses are huge, stone walls reaching up into the sky, blocking out the bright sun—but not blocking out this light, the light of the desert. Across the road, sitting on a wall, my friend waves to me. He has been waiting a long time. I draw close and look into his face, that long-loved face of friendship. His eyes twinkle, and he smiles as if to say, "Finally! You've arrived!" My face is gone, emptied out of me like the contents of a bucket turned upside down, and in the space remaining shines the light.

The light. It is like a fire, burning away my appearance, burning away my bones, burning away my being. And in the ashes, like a phoenix rising, is my friend's face.

"Come on," he says, jumping down from the wall. "Let's go for a ride." We walk over to his car and get in. He glances at me, smiling, and then turns the key in the ignition. It is a half-car, the back end bitten off and swallowed by the desert. He releases the brake and presses his foot down on the accelerator. Slowly, beyond the windshield, the houses begin to slide toward us, expanding until they are bigger than the sky, then slipping off the edge of the world into the fire. The road ahead is like a rope shaken from side to side, or a snake held by the tail, twisting and straightening, twisting and straightening as it picks up speed and disappears into the fire. Trees grow in seconds from tiny sticks into looming giants, as if movement is force-growing them before tossing them into the fire. Even the sun, riding the clouds, swings back and forth across the sky, dipping in and out of the fire like a doughnut dunked in acid and then magically reconstituted.

Here, however, in the fire, we sit, cool. I feel as if I am in a movie theatre watching a car race filmed from the passenger's seat. I am not moving. The theatre is not moving. Even the car—the half-car—is not moving, its hood like a ship's prow projecting firmly into the waves of world that rush past and break upon the sands of the desert, draining away into stillness.

"Where are we going?" I ask.

I look around. The sands of the desert, the light and the fire and the vast emptiness, have engulfed me

30

and covered up my path. No signposts survive here; no guide points the way.

"We're already there," he replies.

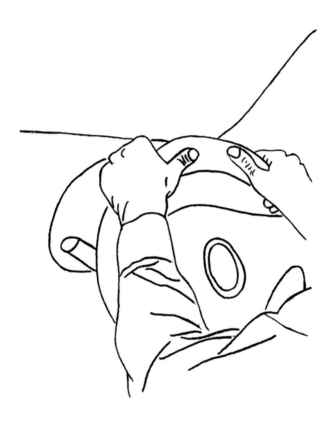

Desert 4

I live in the desert—this no-face, no-place, emptiness here. Among friends in rooms, laughing, I hear the desert. By the reservoir, alone, stars wobbly dots of light in the black water, I see the desert. Hand-in-hand beside the river where the swans nest and the tall flags of yellow iris turn white under the full moon, I walk in the desert.

Today, I follow the path beside the river of yellow irises. At the footbridge, I climb over the railing and sit on a ledge near the surface of the water, facing downstream. My feet dangle over the rushing bubbles where the water flows forcefully around the concrete piling. Above my feet is my belly, above my belly, my chest, above my chest, this desert, vast and empty, out of which pours splashing and tumbling the river on its way to the sea.

Leaving the desert, I return to it, drawn by an instinctive urge for the feel of it, for its space and freedom, like a swallow taking wing in a far country to return again to these wooden eaves and the wide, swooping skies of summer. How many times I have journeyed here under this compulsion, following the path of my shirt buttons till it peters out and I look once more into emptiness. Like a fool, I have stood on street corners, cars honking, shoppers hurrying, working my way in from the edges of the city, in from the buildings and the road and the people and the machines, in from the sound and the movement, in toward myself till I am gone, my appearance plucked out of me like a house sucked up by a tornado, and in my stead, discovered, here, once more, the still and silent desert.

And so when finally I flew across Europe and took a bus south into the Sinai Desert and saw for the first time the sand, the rocks strewn across the flatness, the wide sky edged in the distance by hills that knew nothing but sun and wind and nights dense with stars and cold, my heart beat fast. Here was the desert—*the* desert, *my* desert, the land I had lived in for so long become color and shape, become tangible, become so real that I was sitting in a bus moving through it. I was in the desert, and the desert was in me, a desert of rock pouring forth from the desert of being. And as the recognition welled up out of the emptiness, I wept. The inner and the outer deserts had become one, and I had come home.

Desert 5

The path of my shirt buttons descends into this desert, this void, this emptiness here and disappears.

I look at the path carefully, like a detective down on hands and knees examining the ground for clues. There is my shirt, rising and falling, the little white buttons marking the path. Slowly, I trace the path with my finger across my belly to my chest, resting my finger on the last visible button. The tip of my finger has become blurred, dissolving in front of my eyes, like feet disappearing into quicksand.

I look around. My shoulders, close to, are also blurred, as if I have entered a country over which a spell has been cast that dissolves the edges of things. My edges.

I look back at my finger and move it one step closer, over the edge. The tip is gone. My head is gone. The path is gone.

I wiggle my finger, dipped into nothingness. At the blurred edge of the path, the knuckle moves. But in the stillness of the desert, all movement has come to rest.

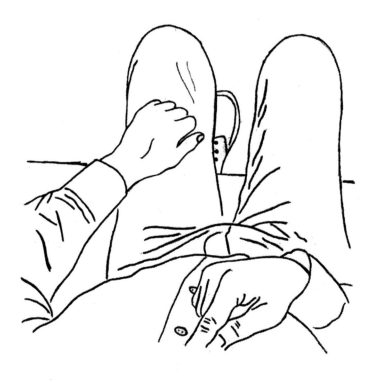

Desert 6

After the workshop with Douglas, I walk into the grounds of the country house. A worn path leads through groves of copper beeches in the full display of summer. I am in shock—gone, demolished, undressed, my appearance removed from me like a sign taken down from a window. I am a vacant lot where once stood a building. I have been blasted out of existence.

My appearance blasted.

My self blasted.

My existence blasted.

Blasted.

Blasted.

Blasted.

And yet the clarity shines—and in the clarity, thick dark trunks reach up, forking into boughs and cascading in a myriad leaves.

I stand for a moment in the soft shadows, my absence full of clarity and trees.

Around a bend in the path appears the wiry man from the workshop. He stops ten feet in front of me, looking at me, observing me. What should I say?

I look at him and speak only one word: "Blasted."

"Ah, yes," he says, looking away for a moment, a frown between his eyes. And then he surprises me.

"You should try being blasted for a year."

A year! A whole year! The thought seems outrageous to me.

But it wasn't, by far.

III

A Seed

Seed 1

On the bare ground, a seed. In the desert. In the emptiness. How can this be? I reach down and pick it up, so small, like a grain of sand, and place it on my open palm. Where could it have come from?

Around me, as far as I can see, is emptiness. No animal moves, not a snake or a desert fox. No plant grows, lodged among rocks. Nothing is here, living or dead.

And yet, I have found a seed. My heart wakes with excitement.

Seeds come from flowers—are blown on the wind, carried by birds, cast by human hands. Moistened, they extend roots and spread leaves, unfurl flowers from tiny buds. They are the future packed tight, secret bouquets of promise and hope.

What promise is hidden within this little seed? Whose promise?

I look up. In the distance, where the hills meet the sky, dark clouds are gathering. Thunder grumbles there, like an old god waking. A cool wind touches my cheek. Rain is coming. Rain is coming.

I hold the seed a little longer, and then drop it upon the ground. It disappears into the sand. For a moment, I am confused. Is the desert a desert of seeds, not sand?

But the rain is approaching fast, sweeping across the plain. I can see it now, charcoal wisps of hair trailing the heavy clouds. A flash of lightning illumines the hills. Thunder cracks, powerful and sharp.

I breathe deep the freshness in the air. The rains will come. The desert will germinate.

Seed 2

I sit on the back step of my house and once again commit myself to living from this emptiness. I will see who is sitting here. I will learn to love from this absence. I will share my self with others.

Who within me is committing myself thus? To whom am I promising myself? The questions are difficult, splitting me into me and Me and snaring me in a spider web of thought.

But my heart is not split. There the yearning rises in a single, simple sensation, like a fountain.

I stand up and walk back into the kitchen. My daughter, Simone, is sitting at the table drawing a picture. I sit next to her and look at the shapes appearing on the paper: a house with a smoking chimney, some flowers, and two kids in front.

"This is Katie's house," she says.

"Is that you and Katie?" I ask, pointing to the two figures.

"Of course," she says. "Who else would it be?"

I pause. Simone adds a red shape next to herself and Katie.

"What is that?" I ask, taking the risk of this being another dumb question.

"That's Katie's cat," she says, and she sighs with

satisfaction. She puts down the crayon and climbs over to my lap.

"Daddy. Tell me a story." I clasp her round the belly and kiss her on the cheek.

"OK. Once upon a time, the end."

"No, a real story," she says.

"OK. Once upon a time, there was a snail called Smudgeon..."

"Smudgeon?" she asks, turning around to look at me. "Who is Smudgeon?"

"I don't know. That's what we're going to find out, isn't it?"

"All right," she says and settles down to listen.

Slowly, the tale unfolds out of the emptiness, like yarn unraveling from an invisible ball of wool. We listen together, intrigued, an audience of two. Yet in the emptiness, the words and images come and go alone.

Seed 3

At dawn, I get out of bed, walk carefully across creaking floorboards so as not to wake my family, and sit on a cushion in the living room. I close my eyes and focus on my breath, counting each exhalation till I reach four and then starting over again at one. It is a simple meditation but difficult, for my attention quickly drifts into memories and images and fears and hopes till I have forgotten all about the breath and the counting. Then suddenly—I don't know why—I remember what I have set out to do, and I focus again on the breath and on the counting.

If this is as far as I go, then I have failed. I have become sidetracked into trying to achieve clarity of mind and have overlooked my true destination, the clarity of no-mind. In the desert, I have committed myself not to my mind nor to my character nor to the strength of my will but to the one source of all these things. I have committed myself to noticing that I am awake in the emptiness.

And so to honor this commitment, I turn from observing the breathing to observing where the breathing is happening. Immediately I am alert. My breathing, I discover, is not happening in my chest. No body encases it. No muscles move it. No blood flows round it. I am astonished: my breathing comes and goes in absolute emptiness.

For a moment I attend to this breathing in emptiness. And then I notice that what is true of the breathing is true also of the counting. A number upturns itself out of nowhere, like the silver side of a fish flashing for a moment in invisible depths. Then the number is gone, not into a mind, but into emptiness, like a soap bubble drifting across a park and suddenly bursting.

I shift my weight on the cushion. A bird sings in the emptiness. My knee aches in the emptiness. Images and memories arise and disappear in the emptiness, like sand falling through my fingers. In the emptiness, I sit and breathe and count with nothing but a naked intent toward the emptiness.

Seed 4

In the afternoon, out walking, I come to a pedestrian bridge spanning railway tracks. I climb the metal steps and walk to the middle of the bridge, stopping to look over the side. Below me two pairs of tracks, pinned to wooden sleepers and shiny with use, disappear under the bridge. Small grey stones fill the spaces between the sleepers, and here and there litter lies—a paper cup, some beer cans, a plastic bag flattened by rain. On the bridge is this empty space, this no-body, this absence looking at things.

I look up, following the lines of the tracks until they meet in a dot on the horizon. Tiny factories sit like distant container ships on either side of the dot, and above them the wide sky climbs to the zenith and then disappears into the emptiness at its edge.

I look at this emptiness. It descends like a huge waterfall from the edge of the sky all the way down to my feet, washing me away and replacing me with the factories, the tracks, the litter, and the bridge.

My eyes fall again on the tiny place where the tracks merge. Something is moving there, a dot, growing slowly, taking shape, its outline expanding like a balloon being blown up. Details appear—the dark dot turning to the yellow of an engine, its front window flashing in the sunlight, bringing with it a rumbling noise, like a fast heart beat, growing louder as the train grows faster down the track, closer and closer till the carriages stretch out behind it and the noise screams everywhere and the face of the driver small but clear looks up from the window, smiling as with the force of thunder the train slams into the emptiness here.

Engulfed by the noise, I swing round to look over the other side of the bridge at the train shooting out of the emptiness, and right there I am hit by a second train slamming big and loud and fast into the emptiness.

On the bridge, destroyed, I watch one train being swallowed up into nothing while the other rushes out of it, shrinking quickly till like a tiny caterpillar it creeps away into the distance. At the center here, all is silence, stillness, and emptiness—the desert.

And yet it is not only the desert. It is also the seed—awake to the explosion of the trains and, unlikely as it sounds, waking to its own emptiness. What power is here in this emptiness, that it can do these impossible things? And what will a life, an ordinary life, my life, grow into when its roots seek, day after day, in the ordinary things of life, awareness of this emptiness?

Seed 5

Each day is a day in the desert—looking, looking. For what am I looking? Mysteriously, I am looking for what is in front, around, and behind me all the time—the desert.

Before work sometimes, I swim in the local pool, opening my eyes under the surface to find blue water everywhere. It fills the emptiness, like an oasis unexpectedly overflowing and spreading across the desert, all the way to the horizon. I move my arms freestyle. One at a time they appear out of nowhere, reaching into the water in front of me. My head, my torso, and my legs are nonexistent—as if upon entering the water I had discarded them like clothes, leaving me naked. My body is now this body of water, within which in the emptiness kicking sensations appear like fish swimming inside me.

This then is my practice: observing the emptiness in each moment of remembering. Like a child crossing the street, I look both ways carefully: in and out. I drive to the station and observe my hands holding the wheel, hands that are joined to arms that are joined not to a body but to the emptiness here. I board the train, and looking down the length of the carriage, observe how small the far end and how big the near end is, opening out into this openness here. I leave the train and ride the escalator up to the street, observing with pleasure the smooth descent of the walls and ceiling into the stillness where I stand. Ostensibly, I am on my way to work. And indeed, the moment does arrive when I withdraw my key from my pocket and, extending my arm, insert the key into the lock in my office door. But this key is only the key to my temporary destination. As I pause and look at it, half-hidden in the lock, my attention travels up my arm to my shoulder and then over the edge of my shoulder into the emptiness. Looking in, I find another key, the key to all my endings and beginnings, my stops and starts, my departures and arrivals; the key to my eternal destination.

Turning the key, I open the door and walk into my office.

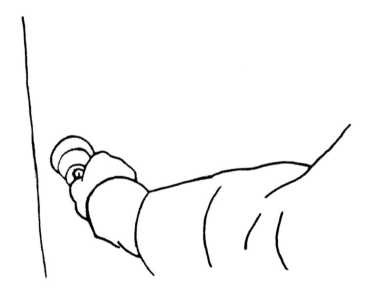

IV

Leaves

Leaves 1

The seed, touched by water, in the dark of the soil sprouts.

At first I see nothing, observing only the bare surface of the soil. But after a week, the tiny stalk pushes away a clump of soil and emerges into the light, bearing two small leaves at its tip like hands held together in prayer. I am excited and tell Carol, sewing at the kitchen table. She comes to look, and we stand together as we have often stood watching Simone playing. Here it is, in our own back yard, life beginning.

Later, sitting on the garden bench, I look at the tomato plants we put in a couple of weeks ago, sturdy six-inch systems of single stems and leaves reaching upward. I imagine time future, summer's midpoint, and see the plants grown large and complex in their greenery, little red bunches hanging where we saw the yellow flowers open. And I wonder about the seed, now this sprout, this search for the sun which is growing—how I don't know—in the soil.

"What kind of seed is it?" Carol asked when I first showed it to her.

"I don't know," I said.

"Let's plant it and find out," said Simone.

And so we did.

And now I sit here watching the leaves unfold—
looking, looking.

Leaves 2

And so the path began, feeling its way from the oak-paneled room and my finger pointing for the first time at emptiness, out through the cascading leaves into the stillness of the desert and the finding of the seed, on into the years of fullness and the years of emptiness and this moment here, in the early morning, writing, the sound of rain dripping from the edge of the roof into this same, unchanging emptiness.

One by one, the leaves unfurl. I remember, only a day or two after that first experience of pointing, or perhaps only a few hours, sitting casually in a group of four or five people from the workshop. We were in one of the lounges of the country house, relaxing in large, easy chairs. At seventeen, I was self-conscious and reticent among adults. But in this room the seventeen-year-old had vanished, and with him had gone his self-consciousness. In his stead I found a simple, peaceful clarity in which, as in a crystal ball, the group sat talking.

I turned to Douglas, sitting next to me. He looked at me, but I felt no embarrassment or fear as I looked into his face. The blue of his eyes was only the blue of his eyes. The white of his beard was only the white of his beard. Where was the Douglas whose gaze would in the past have intimidated me? Nowhere. For that Douglas appeared to have been imaginary, dissolved in the clarity here and replaced by the real Douglas there, all colors and shapes and feelings and sounds—and nothing else. I imagined no judge sitting behind his eyes. I looked and found only Douglas, my new friend, on full display in my absence.

I looked at the others in the group. It was the same. My fear of them had gone along with my head. I was empty, and the emptiness was open, and the openness held their faces as if newly created—the pink in their cheeks, the laughter in their eyes, the easygoing looks at me and at each other. A feeling, strange yet familiar, stirred in me. Here were people whom I barely knew and who were much older than I, yet I felt quickly, deeply connected to them. I felt, even, that I had known them before, that they were old friends. How could this be? I looked at the man with the hooked nose, and he smiled easily. And surprised, I understood. We *were* old friends, friends from even before time began. For in these faces I recognized the smile of the Friend within us all.

And yet something was missing, and I felt disturbed. Though lovely, these people appeared two-dimensional. They were like cardboard cutouts, like moving, talking, paper dolls. The woman with the large smile looked at me. Her face was generous and open, but it was flat. Her head had no depth, no sides or back to it. It was as thin as a photograph. After a moment, she turned to talk to the person next to her, and her face became one-eyed, a profile pasted onto the wall behind her.

Was this woman only a surface among surfaces? Had the vision of my emptiness emptied her of her three-dimensional reality?

I looked back at Douglas. What I had noticed about the others was also true of him. He too was flat. And his flatness allowed no room for an inner self. Douglas, alive, intelligent, friendly—and two-dimensional—was all surface. No space existed within him for consciousness.

I stared at my no-face. The world I saw here in this room had left the path of the world I had matured in, the world on which my values and beliefs rested. I had lost my appearance and had become all consciousness, but these people seemed to have lost their consciousnesses and become all appearance. I had been promoted to the infinite and eternal subject, but they had been demoted to small, temporary objects among other temporary objects. Wasn't this view dangerous—narcissistic, solipsistic, even perhaps totalitarian in its assertion that people were things? Didn't it threaten the humanity of people?

Yet the feeling in the group was loving and respectful.

Later, as the months and years of exploration came and went, I returned again and again to this problem, trying to understand. I could *see* that people had no room within them for consciousnesses. Yet they often assured me that they *were* conscious, sometimes agreeing that they were made of emptiness, too, like me. In London, living with a group of people who shared this way of *seeing*, I would look long into a friend's face as she looked into mine. I traveled with my eye the country of her features—her smooth forehead, on which fell ringlets of dark hair, her hazel irises, her warm, quick smile wrinkling the corners of her eyes and bringing the color to her cheeks. How lovely was this looking, how relaxed, her face in my absence, the absence seeming to grow more clear upon inspection until it was an empty mirror in which the face I was looking at became, in fact, my own. For again, I perceived no *her* behind her face to own it. Nowhere in or behind her face could I find her consciousness.

And yet how could I deny it? For she would tell me what *she* saw—her own headless awareness clear as a mirror, my face within her infinitude slowly dropping its disguise as the face of another person until she recognized it to be, in these moments of looking, the face of her own self.

Where, I wondered, could her headless awareness be? Where could it be hidden? The idea that it was inside her head was as unsupportable as the idea that her personal consciousness was there. Apart from the fact that her face was flat appearance, an infinite awareness could not fit inside a head. Nor did *she* claim that her awareness was inside her head. It was, she said, like mine, uncontained and free.

I was stalled in contradiction and confusion.

And then one day, years later, I walked into a large grocery store in California. Standing in the entrance way several steps above the main floor, I looked out over the crowd of small, two-dimensional shoppers. As usual, I perceived my own consciousness here in me but perceived no other consciousnesses inside or behind the appearances of the shoppers. And the problem presented itself again. Was I the only consciousness? Were these people, busy picking vegetables and fruit from the wooden bins, simply without consciousness?

Then the obvious hit me smack in the face. Of course! How silly I had been, trying in confusion to figure out where hidden consciousnesses could be or thinking that people were not conscious. They were obviously conscious. But their consciousness was not *behind* or *within* them. It was *in front* of them, all over the store, one wide, open, shared, aware space. It couldn't have been more on show or less hidden. This space I was looking at or with was what the shoppers were looking at or with also—the very same, directly! It was their awareness as well as mine, our unified, eternal, infinite act of looking. What a surprise, like coming by chance upon one's closest friend in a foreign country. "This is you! This is you!" I shouted silently to them. I looked at a face in the openness and stared at our identical consciousness. I turned to another face and perceived the same. The consciousness of one person was not separate from the consciousness of another, and neither was separate from this consciousness here. No lines divided it. No names claimed it. No appearances concealed it. Each shopper moved around this shared consciousness like fish swimming within the sea.

I type on the computer, watching the words and images materialize out of nowhere. The morning— this one bright with sunshine—rises from behind the neighbor's house. I am alone, and yet I enjoy here the consciousness of everyone I have ever and never met, finding in this awake absence the undisguised face of the Friend who is everywhere.

Leaves 3

We stand in a circle, arms around each other's waists, looking down. On the floor are eight pairs of shoes. Eight bodies rise from the shoes like the petals of a flower—legs, bellies, chests. But at the top of the circle, not eight heads look down. Not even one head. Instead, above the blurred edge of each chest is one no-headed emptiness. Not my emptiness next to your emptiness. Not edges and names. Only indefinable awareness looking down at eight headless bodies.

Is this, perhaps, a caterpillar—one being with many legs that bears within it the secret butterfly of love?

Down there on the carpet I look and see the land of feet, the land of comings and goings, the land of hellos and goodbyes. These feet that stand together there will shortly depart, travelling in many directions on paths that eventually will lead to death as surely as they began with birth. For down there is also the land of births and deaths, the land of the comings and goings of our mortal selves.

But here at the top of the circle are no heads, no feet, no comings and goings, no hellos followed by goodbyes. Here is no birth followed by death, for nothing exists here to be born or to die. Here instead is a mysterious land—pure emptiness and awareness—the land of the eternal birth and the eternal hello.

Slowly, I look up. Each headless body around me grows a head, like the boughs of a tree miraculously producing fruit. How beautiful are these faces!

I count seven heads. One is missing—between the face on my left and the face on my right—its place and life surrendered so that in the midst of these friends the one Friend may be present.

We drop our arms, and separate, and say goodbyes. I close the door after the last has left and sit in an easy chair, looking at this clarity. The appearances have gone, but their reality has not. I look at it and greet my friends once again in the one who always seems to be arriving but who never, ever leaves.

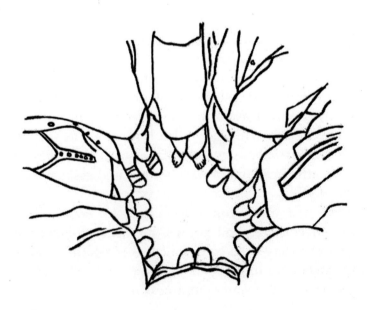

Leaves 4

On a wooden bench in the parking lot of a fast food place, I sit. Behind me is a jungle of ropes, slides, and tunnels which the management has installed to attract travelers like my six-year-old daughter, Simone, and me on long car trips. A sign at the entrance to this jungle features a grinning brown monkey about four feet high hanging from the limb of a tree. The monkey is blowing a blue bubblegum balloon, inside of which are the words, "If you are taller than me, you cannot enter the jungle." I am taller than the monkey, and I obey him. So does my daughter. She is in there somewhere in the deeps of play. And I am here on the bench in the sunshine, facing the cars in the lot and, beyond the lot, the soft brown California hills, the color of late summer.

The sunlight is startlingly bright, conferring an immediacy on the cars in front of me, on the black tarmac, and, I see it now, on the emptiness here in which they miraculously appear. The rows of smooth, late-model cars glint, some ticking quietly as their engines cool. I look up. The sky is deep blue. Beyond the hills I imagine the ocean, cool and tumultuous, but I cannot feel it. The hills basket the heat. Above the hills are the sky and the sun and, at the limits of vision, this intensely cool and mysterious wakefulness.

I look to my left and see from where I sit the fast food establishment, a low glass-and-wood building with an overhanging roof of red tile. The glass door in the center swings outward, pushed from within by a small, white-haired, overweight man. He is wearing a light cotton jacket, blue jeans, and white running shoes. Letting go of the door, he stops to squint for a moment in the sunlight and then ambles in my direction across the short, concrete patio and down the three steps to the tarmac of the lot. He has the gait of one who has fed well and who is enjoying the feel of the food in his stomach.

As he approaches, I observe him closely. And I observe myself, the empty but inquisitive stage across which he is walking. Gradually, his body expands, like a balloon slowly inflating. His face, grown big like a full moon, rises above the roof of the building behind him, heading for the sun. His girth obscures one, now two, cars from my sight. He has gained the stature of a giant, yet no awareness of this momentous change shows on his face. He seems still to be enjoying quietly the weight of his meal.

Suddenly he is passing in front of me. I try to see his face, but the brightness of the sun next to it dazzles me. I look away for relief, down to the black tarmac, and find, frozen in the moment, two pairs of legs, his and mine, and that is all. His legs, in mid-stride, are surmounted by a belly, above which is nothing but the pristinely empty awareness. My legs, bent in alertness and yet strangely anonymous, are also surmounted by a belly and fade off into the same indivisible emptiness. We have merged in nothingness, dropped together into an infinite White Rabbit's hole in the parking lot, at one with each other unintroduced and without acknowledging to each other that we are one.

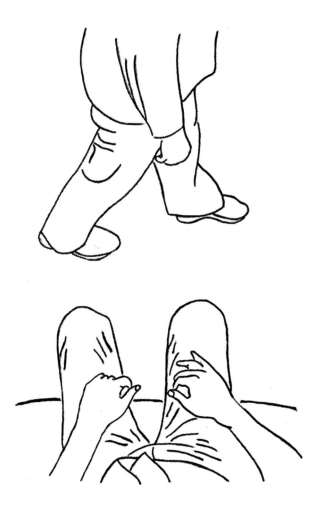

Then, though the moment seems timeless, the moment is over. I look at his back as he moves away from me, his body shrinking in a kind of Doppler goodbye until he turns beside a row of cars and slips unobtrusively into a tiny, invisible slit between the bits of the universe.

"Daddy! Watch me!" I turn around and peer into the lacework of ropes that looks like a prison and a sailship crammed into a box of colors. I cannot see Simone. She is an animal hidden in this jungle, camouflaged in play. "Here I am," she calls in a high voice. I follow the voice and see her waving to me, her bright face looking over the edge of an orange, tubular slide on top of the structure. And then she is gone. I trace closely with my eye the snaking tunnel to work out where she will appear next. But before I have reached its end, she shoots out of nowhere very close to me, her eyes catching fire from her smile.

"Ah, there you are!" I say, grinning. But she is gone again, into the jungle, laughing.

Leaves 5

To walk across the living room floor into the kitchen and to observe as I do so that I am infinite—I marvel at it. How can I extend without limits? And yet I do. I go on and on for ever.

When I try to think about this infinity, I am stunned. Thoughts go with things that have edges, with concepts that can be defined. I have no difficulty, for example, thinking about the kitchen. I can draw a line around it, separating it from the living room on one side and the laundry on the other, and so define it. Nor, in principle, do I have difficulty thinking about abstractions like "good." I can draw a mental line around the concept, separating it from what is "bad," and so define it. But when I try to express in words the infinity which I see here so easily, I stumble. I can draw no lines around it. Outside the edges to which words attach themselves, it is indefinable.

The word "infinite" itself suggests this problem of expression, for broken into its parts, it means "non-finite" or "without edges." It is thus a word that acknowledges its own limits, as if it can only look at the world and say, "I do not refer to these edges. Infinity is not this." Thus it cannot say what infinity is, only what it is not.

What, then, can I think about infinity? Nothing. My thoughts stall repeatedly against the wall of their own limitations. But when at the same time I look into infinity, my awareness leaps over that wall and runs beyond it, immeasurably beyond it, unbelievably and impossibly and inconceivably beyond it, shouting with astonishment and joy at the perception that I am marvelously and infinitely free.

Leaves 6

Sitting at my desk at work, between tasks, the word "infinity" comes to mind, and so I look again into infinity. How easily and simply, I think, does this looking at what I see shed light on difficult questions. Take, for example, the question, Is there an edge to the universe? The idea that the edge of the universe could be found by my looking for it in my office would cause some light-hearted laughter among my colleagues, who would doubtless suggest that in looking for that edge in room 563, I had already gone over it. But why should the edge, if it exists, be far away, out there in the cosmos beyond the reach of perception? Why must it be an abstraction, understood only by mathematicians, if, even, by them? Perhaps, I speculate, it only has to be an abstraction if one looks for it only among abstractions.

And so I sit back and, despite the imagined merriment of my colleagues, look for the edge of the universe from my office chair.

What do I find? In front of me, my desk abuts against a wall of shelves, thick with books and binders. Continuing to look straight ahead, I see the walls to the left and right joining the wall in front. The left wall is concrete and white; the right is opaque glass with a green wooden door, half open at the edge nearest to me. But these three walls are all that I can see. I see no fourth wall linking them behind, closing me in.

Without turning my head, I look more closely at the near ends of these side walls, using my peripheral vision. The ends of the walls are blurred. Their shape and color and texture blend together. Right at the edge of my field of vision, the walls are almost indefinable, mere splodges of amorphous color. And then, beyond these splodges, nothingness, emptiness, infinity.

Here, then, in this indeterminate part of my office, I have found the edge of the universe. It is a band where thingness merges across no hard line into no-thingness. Like a tiny star which I can see only if I look askance at it, the edge declines direct observation. And yet, out of the corner of my eye, I *can* see it—see on one side of it the frayed edge of my office and on the other, the void.

What happens if I approach this edge? I turn to the right, and out of the edge on the right moves the fourth wall, at first blurred but becoming clearer until it is in front of me, stacked with two tall black file cabinets and a bookcase. The edge, however, has not moved. Nor in fact have I, for I notice now again that I have no head to move. Instead, quietly, easily, new parts of the room have slid out of the blurred edge. Here in my office, overlooked a thousand times a day, is the universe's birthplace, the fecund emptiness where things materialize out of nothingness via a zone where they are not quite things and not quite nothingness. Here, open to direct observation, is the ongoing creation of matter.

And the ongoing destruction of matter. For as things materialize on one side of the room, they dematerialize on the other, going through the same band of indeterminacy in reverse order. Here in the midst of me is a black hole, absorbing into the timeless and spewing forth into time the objects of my office, the Quiet Crunch and the Quiet Bang happening over and over concurrently, and happening again now as I turn back to face my desk.

It seems, then, that I cannot quite reach the universe's edge, cannot bring it into focus. Like a rainbow which retreats always from the traveler seeking the pot of gold at its end, the edge remains at the edge of my vision. It is the permanent edge.

Yet, strangely, I can look over it. And in looking over it, I seem to step over it into the nothingness. It is a paradoxical nothingness, inconceivably vast and at the same time tinier than a quark, in the end immeasurable because the ruler I use to measure it itself dissolves in the nothingness. It is a placeless place, empty of markers, a blankness so blank that I cannot even call it a blank. What is beyond the edge of the universe? Illogically, nothing at all.

But that is only half the answer. For as soon as I put my foot into the airy emptiness beyond the edge of the universe, my shoe touches—surprise, surprise—the floor of my office. Beyond the edge of my office is not just an emptiness but an emptiness full of my office. I feel as if I am walking along a giant Moebius strip: what is inside seamlessly becomes what is outside, and what is outside seamlessly becomes what is inside. Or I have suddenly turned without knowing how into a magician who, in full view of the audience, makes a coin simultaneously disappear from one hand and reappear in the other.

My office is rounded with a nothingness, like a picture without a frame on a non-existent wall. Where, I wonder, did the picture come from? Who hung it up? And what holds it there, wherever 'there' might be?

Is there an edge to the universe?

I look and see.

Leaves 7

The doorbell rings. I open the door and see my friend standing there, smiling in the empty frame of the doorway.

"Want to go for a spin?"

I remember the time he drove me through countryside at night with his headlights off, just for the thrill of it. But the sun is up now. I get my jacket.

We head out of town across the river, between fields of rough, yellow stubble and up into the hills. The road becomes steep, blinkered with high hedges that whiz by in a blur. At the top of the hill, we park and get out of the car. The view is miles wide, a far flatness of farmland in the middle of which is the river, sunning itself like a snake. The air and land lie together in the still haze of noon.

We turn from the view and walk along the edge of the hill. A path finds us, and we follow it between tall, purple-flowering weeds. Gravel crunches under our feet. Birdsong seeks us out, its source hidden.

The path veers left, and suddenly in front of us is a Norman keep, a tall round tower of tan-colored stone, dating from the twelfth century. Its walls are worn but complete. Slits high up served once as defensive lookouts, hard to penetrate with arrows but well suited for launching them.

We walk up close and touch the tower, running our hands over its surface. The stone is cold in the shadows, warm in the sun, its texture uneven—smooth here, rough there, the valleys in it a record of the rain that has fallen down the centuries, down the hard, resisting weight of stone.

Around the side, we find a doorway about the size of a large man. We pass through, and I notice with surprise the thickness of the wall—four feet at least. Inside, the tower looks smaller than from outside. The space is empty, swept clean, open to the sky. My friend walks across to the opposite wall and leans against it. He is tall, easy-limbed, relaxed.

I stand in the middle of this circle of stone, this fortress which has withstood the assault of eight hundred years. It seems to be sleeping, heavy with dreams.

I begin to turn clockwise, like a dervish in slow motion. Or rather, the fortress begins to move from right to left across this unmoving clarity. The doorway appears, sliding out of nowhere into the center of my vision and then sliding off into the stillness. My friend appears, still leaning against the wall, but moving also with the wall. Then he is gone, chasing the door. I turn faster. The walls pick up speed. The door appears again, and then my friend, and then the wall, and then again the door and my friend again, swinging through the stillness like children clinging to a spinning carousel. Faster still, and the blur of the edge of the world creeps into the world, merging the colors and shapes together in a sweep of movement till all is blurred except this clarity, this stillness here, which seems to grow ever more still and clear, and into which I relax, deeper and deeper, until I am completely still, at rest, at one with the unsleeping stillness at the heart of the stone itself.

Leaves 8

Night. A mountain bluegrass festival. Above, the stars. Around, silhouettes of trees and dancers. In front, the stage, a cave of lights in the dark from which the musicians cast their spell upon the crowd. How strong it is, the energy of the sound. I can almost touch it there, tumbling from the speakers. No, not from the speakers—from the source, from the emptiness, from the silence directly. The dam between this world and the real has broken, and music is bursting through.

I listen to the silence from which the music pours. It is the silence that moves me, the beat and my body dancing in it together, swaying and turning in the stillness. I do not think *how* I should move. The music is my moves, a wild river rushing and laughing in the silence.

Then in the middle of this freedom, I imagine for a moment how free I must look to others around me. Instantly I am awkward and self-conscious. I cannot move with the music anymore. I try to make my body jump, but it feels mechanical. It only goes through the motions, as if I am directing it from outside. In imagining myself in the eyes of others, I have lost the secret of the dance.

And so, at a loss, I stop, and stand, and give up

trying to move, and turn once more to the stillness and the silence.

Immediately, the source pours through me again, and I find in surprise my body in motion, riding the river of song. I am danced, and with me all are danced, and the trees and stars, and the vast night sky, gyrating within the stillness to the beat of the powerful sound.

I listen to the silence and watch the music take me wherever it will go.

Leaves 9

The leaves unfurl slowly with the years. What plant is growing here? What shape might it be taking?

I am not a botanist. I hesitate even over the names of plants I should know well. They slip away from me, leaving me only with colors and patterns, variegated textures to enjoy.

But with this plant—even the names I am sure of seem slippery. Emptiness-Fullness. Silence. Stillness. Infinity. Their number suggests it is ubiquitous, like a wild, wind-sown plant, tall and purple-flowering, though no buds yet show.

I have heard other names for it, too—divine names. God. Allah. The One. Buddha Nature and Atman-Brahman. Being and Consciousness. Such august names. For what? For this no-face, no-place emptiness here?

Perhaps.

Sometimes I see it in my dreams. Like a magic herb, it shows me even then that I have no head. I wonder if this vision is a sign that awareness of emptiness has reached down into my subconscious. That the roots are taking hold.

Taking hold of what? Of emptiness? Of the desert? Of God? The God whom at age sixteen I despaired of ever finding?

Perhaps.

When I first came to the United States, I worked for a while as a busboy in a café. I was twenty-seven with a fine degree and plenty of hopes and no work experience worth speaking of. Collecting dirty dishes, wiping off tables, and sweeping and mopping the floor brought in a little money, and at the same time I practiced seeing this no-face. But that hardly justified the job. Increasingly, I was unable to see how what I was doing fitted into my dreams. I began to get depressed.

Then late one winter afternoon, I was sitting at a table in the café eating a sandwich in my break, the café quiet with the soft lights on for the approaching evening, and suddenly, out of nowhere, clear as if someone were standing behind me, I heard a voice say, "David, you are doing the right thing."

I looked around, startled, for who would say such a thing in a café in so matter-of-fact a tone of voice? But nobody was there. No-one in the café had spoken.

A leaf unfurling? A dream? A root reaching the rich nutrients of the subconscious mind? Was this my God finally, finally speaking to me in a voice that I could hear?

I don't know.

But the clarity of that voice has rung down the years with a mysterious, encouraging sound.

V

Roots

Roots 1

Leaves and flowers decorate my garden. I love to trace their outlines on white paper, seeing them appear like magic on the blankness, forming and growing and cascading in intricate patterns down the empty page. I do not see nor draw the roots. But without those roots, invisible in the dark earth, neither leaves nor flowers nor stems could ever grow.

When I was a gardener, I saw many roots. Roots of weeds, long and pale, which I pulled from the soil. Roots of new plants in tight balls which, removed from containers and scored or spread, I placed carefully in the ground. Roots of trees round which I dug to install irrigation systems. How purposeful they were, searching thick darkness for nutrients and water so that stems could strengthen against the wind, leaves unfurl into sunlight, flowers unfold to bees and human eyes.

But where, I wondered, were *my* roots?

I look now at my body sitting in this chair. It appears inverted, feet pointing towards the top of the picture, belly in the middle, broad shoulders at the bottom. Below the shoulders, below the wide base of this body-mind tree whose whole, spreading, leafy structure is the universe itself, what do I find? No roots, no water, no soil, no searching purpose or will—not even the empty desert. In the place out of which I grow, I find nothing at all.

Who am I that, rooted in nothingness, yet grow? Who am I that, empty of purpose, yet find purpose in searching this emptiness? Who am I that, not even existing, yet sit here comfortably and write these words about my own non-existence?

Roots 2

We sit around, the three of us, talking about our absence.

"And yet what is strangest," he says, "is that when I listen to your voice, I hear it rising out of the same silence as mine."

"Me too," she says. "My absence speaks, and it's the same absence speaking as yours."

"Just as strange," I say, "is that the one who speaks is also the one who listens."

"That *is* strange. I'm speaking with three voices, but I'm only one speaker and listener. Yet, even though I'm the speaker, I still listen closely when I speak because I don't know what I'll say next, whichever voice I use, including this one. It's intense."

"Yes, isn't it? And the listening is stronger when I listen to the silence, as if I'm right there at the source of every word, not an inch away."

"Right. The voices—their timbre and their cadence—are so intimate, so familiar. Each voice is my voice."

"Yet each personal and distinct. How lovely it is to listen and speak like this."

The conversation pauses, though not the listening. In the absence is the presence—awake and tangible.

"So who is this speaker-listener?"

"Who is asking?"

We laugh. The joke is on me, of course.

And yet the question is a real one. I hear it in the listening—to voices, to music, to the noise of traffic, itself another voice. I hear it asked in beauty, in the silence in which birds, and airplanes, sing. In the vast emptiness behind the distant barking of a dog. Everywhere is the listener one with the speaker. And everywhere in the listening and the speaking is the question: Who is this one who hears, who speaks, who listens to itself listening to itself? Who is this strangely awake one, this silence wise enough to be dumbfounded at its own non-existence? Who, I ask, again and again and again, speaking in every voice and listening in every sound, who, who, who am I?

Roots 3

On the beach, I sit and watch Carol and Simone playing store with shells and sand. They are absorbed in the game, crouching, talking, oblivious to the seagulls standing nearby and to the quiet ripple of the tide, oblivious to my presence on this blanket. They are so real, so solid, so purposeful in the intricacies of their make-believe. And I? A vapor, a cloud, an airy nothingness. Not even a presence but an absence.

Out of the corner of my eye, I see a seagull edge toward the basket of food. I look at the bird directly. Its belly is pure white, its folded wings a soft blue-grey, its beak, slightly hooked, yellow and dangerous looking. The bird stops a few feet away, nervous, ready to pounce or fly.

Beyond the bird I see other birds, other beach goers, the clouds, the sun—all real, all present. But I—a nothingness, insubstantial, inconsequential. Yet I am a nothingness that knows it is a nothingness.

Carol breaks from the game and looks up, smiling.

"Are you hungry?" she asks.

I am. We all are. I grab the basket, my hand reaching out of the nothingness. The seagull rises on the air, squawking, its huge wings flapping.

We eat. I watch my food descend to the edge

of the world and then disappear into this waking non-existence.

Roots 4

I shut my eyes like a toddler performing a trick. The room vanishes. I open my eyes. The room appears. Where does it go? From where does it return? Emptiness? Absence? Nothingness? What are these?

I look down at my body. Who is looking down without a head? No-one. And yet this no-one, this nothingness, looks down.

Is this then who I am—a nothingness that sees?

And wonders at itself. For what does this nothingness see? Not only a room and a body but also itself—nothingness. Surely this is impossible. How can nothingness see nothingness?

And yet I do.

Roots 5

Where have I come from? Where am I going?

Having no edges, I can find no answer to these questions. How, extending into infinity, could I have come from anywhere else? Where on earth could I be going? All my horizons are imaginary, all my origins unfounded.

I leave the house before anyone else is awake and walk through the woods to the river, standing on the cliff and looking out across the wide waters. Geese in long, spidery formations fly in from the emptiness, honking in the early morning air, and head up river, exiting into my non-existence. They come and they go, so straightforwardly. But I—I have never seen myself arrive or leave anywhere. Nothing of me moves, is born, sprouts, dies. Have I always been like this?

I take the path along the edge of the cliff. The large old oak, burly, its branches thick and stunted with the vicissitudes of age, leans out over the steep, far drop to the river's beach. Its roots are half exposed, the tension of its grip into the crumbling cliff obvious. Within a decade, the earth will release it, and with a terrifying noise the tree will crash down to the water's edge, lying there for years afterwards a gigantic log, its high limbs reachable even by small children, its roots displayed for everyone to see. How things with edges all have beginnings and endings. And how I have none of these.

The path takes me further along the cliff and then down through ferns and trees to the river. I stand for a moment and listen to the soft lapping of the water, so gentle in the silence, and then turn and walk along the beach until I come to where I always aim to come upon these walks: the avenue of trees. They are so tall, with roots, I imagine, extending deep into the earth. I touch the bark of the nearest tree and look up into its branches. On the highest limbs, gold and orange from the rising sun have already alighted, waiting yet to descend to me. I look down. The base of the broad trunk merges into the earth, and I imagine again the roots stretching deep and wide in the darkness of soil and rocks, interweaving with the roots of the other trees, listening for the quiet trickle of water. In my mind, I seem to enter this underground realm and feel my way into these roots—cool, searching, stable, while far above the surface of the soil unnoticed winds may sway branches and tear off leaves.

As if to join more closely with these roots, I lie down on my back at the base of the tree. Looking up, I see again the glowing branches. Looking down—and in—I gaze not at a person, nor at soil, nor at imagined roots, but stare instead into the absence of these things—clarity, emptiness, pure wakefulness. Who is looking, the tree or I? I do not know. The tree rises out of the limpidity I am as if out of a perfectly clear pool of awareness. But out of what, I wonder, does the awareness rise? From where does the pool spring? I cannot say. Neither tree nor I nor awareness has any roots, or soil, or rocks, or any source from which we can take our being. Here is no cliff to cling to, no beach to crash upon, no place that awareness can point to and say, "This is where I came from; this is where I am going." I seem to float, without origin or destination, and with no explanation, in the absence of who I am.

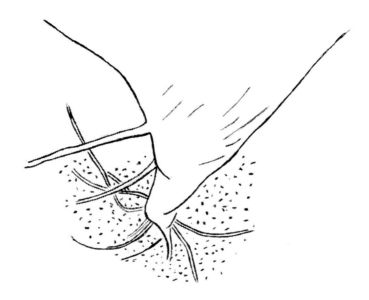

VI

Cold and Heat

Cold and Heat 1

At night, the desert is cold, very cold. I wander in its immensity, a blanket wrapped closely around my body. I can see no landmarks. Only the stars in a vast dome of darkness are visible. But I am not a navigator. I cannot read them.

Shivering, I sit on a rock and try to build a fire, smashing stones together. A few sparks fly, floating up into the darkness like shooting stars, but nothing catches fire. My mind plays tricks on me, imagining the sparks to be the eyes of animals waiting for me to weaken. I am afraid.

In the day, the desert I have suffered through at night vanishes. At first, I am relieved. The darkness thins on the eastern horizon, and the stars diminish until only Venus remains, a silver orb shining in the dawn sky. Then even it is gone, dissolved in azure, and the sun, streaking bands of light, rises over the distant edge of the desert, dispersing what is left of the dark, warming my bones.

But the respite is short. The sun climbs the sky, broadening and brightening until it engulfs the whole desert with its heat and light. I throw the blanket off, squinting, my head hot, throat parched, skin burning. Where is the cold now? I long for caves and rain but see only the endless, dry flatness and the intolerable sun. I sift sand through my fingers. I lift up stones. But even there the vagrant shadows have been defeated, the coolness banished. I reach for the blanket and hold it above my head to shield me from the sun. What else can I do?

Cold and Heat 2

Sometimes I dream I have murdered someone but can't remember who or when it was. I do not tell what I have done. I eat meals with friends and go to work as usual. But inside of me, a fugitive runs down back alleys with an overwhelming sense of dread. I have done the worst possible thing: I have killed a person. How did it happen? Whom did I kill? I do not know. But I am guilty, and all that I have striven for in my life I have destroyed.

When I wake from this dream, I do so slowly. Anxiety is everywhere. But as I recognize the dawn glimmering through the curtains, the dream weakens. With relief I realize that I have not actually killed anyone. I am not really a murderer.

I get up, make tea, prepare to leave for work. And yet an element of the dream still lingers, mixing with the light, making me feel I have a reprieve only until the next night comes.

What does this dream mean? Is it just a nightmare, the usual stress of a life in progress? Or is something awful and dangerous happening to me?

I walk the headless way so trustingly. How easy and rich it seems in the day—pointing my finger at emptiness, edging out into infinity, celebrating my nothingness. I reach the mountain top and stand amazed: I am awake, gone without trace. And yet when night enters my heart, I am on no pleasant outing. It is no game. In the act of seeing, I behead myself. Do I understand the consequences? Do I know what I am doing?

Cold and Heat 3

When my heart sinks. When in the night I wake and
fears creep into my mind. When my life goes in the
wrong direction, into failure, into the cul-de-sac of
pressure and disappointment, into nightmare. When
the true extent of my smallness presents itself to me,
and encloses me, and drags me down, and holds me
down, and blinds me, and paralyzes me. Then what
worth this nothingness? What worth this emptiness
waking? Only a comfortless, sterile bowl for my pain.

Unable to sleep, I step out into the night. How the
stars are hidden by it. How, when I walk in the small
hours through the yellow streetlight and head across
the empty town, how I am back again on the moor,
a twelve-year-old crying and alone. I don't know why
this happens. I am familiar with these streets. I know
where I am going—beyond the dark houses to the
Meadow, that broad expanse of grass inhabited by cows
and horses and framed on one side by the soft-flowing
river. But all I feel is dark. Dark infused with dread and
loneliness.

I cross the bridge over the railway tracks, leaving the
houses and the lights, and follow the road in darkness
till it deadends at the gate to the Meadow. I touch the
gate as though I am reaching for it under a blanket and

touch is all I have. Pushing open the clasp, I walk into wider darkness. I hear the gravel of the path crunch under my feet. I hear the snorting of the horses. But no birds sing.

Where am I going, now that I have arrived?

I turn to the emptiness, but all it does is push toward me the pain in my heart.

I walk on further into the Meadow, unseeing, my feet picking out the path. I try to withdraw from the dark into the shell of myself, but the emptiness is cruel. It erases all my edges, embracing the dark, inviting it into every secret corner of my being, laying me out on a slab for all my fears to feed on. I become a country populated by demons, each attacking the others.

I lose track of time. The air suddenly becomes cooler. And then I hear the unceasing rush on the edge of the Meadow. The sound grows till I stand within the invisible roar. I had forgotten this: the weir. I imagine the black water at my feet rolling over the steep concrete edge and falling further into the dark. And I am afraid—afraid that my heart, too, already weighted down, will be sucked over the edge, falling, falling, falling, for ever falling into dark.

Cold and Heat 4

The phone rings. A voice, gentle, oh too gentle, tells me that in England, this morning, now, on this the shortest day of the year, my friend is dead.

How can this be? How can that lithe form which I followed over the Irish hills and down to the seal-bobbing bay, in body and in mind, be gone? Be wiped out, be emptied of laughter and love, be stilled and laid out for identification in the cold of a morgue drawer? How can this be?

His promise—to cross the ocean and the continent and to arrive one day on my doorstep and there to place a pair of traveling boots for me, so that we might once again go into the adventure together—broken in the breaking of his heart. And in the breaking of his heart, my heart is broken, and weeps, and can see no other path than that which would take me to wherever he has gone.

In the evening, a candle burns near his picture. We sit in the edges of the dark, crying. I would give away this whole stupid emptiness to bring him back again.

Cold and Heat 5

I get angry sometimes. So angry. The feeling ignites and flares across the space as if it were gasoline vapor sparked. In the heat I speak or shout without constraint, and someone as well as I gets hurt. At other times I am reserved and speak quietly or do not speak at all. I used to think reason and balance were my guides, but beneath these surfaces, burned away by the insistent heat, I have come to see fear, and resentment, and meanness, and mistrust, making their home in me like demons worming their way into my heart.

I know all this, or think I do, and yet nothing changes. Thirty years in the desert has not reformed my character. Thus doubt about this *seeing* enters my heart, also. Is the headless way only a perceptual reconnaissance of what is so much deeper than the perceptual? Have I stopped short at the evidence of the senses? Sure, I have explored the emptiness extending without extension to infinity. Sure, I have moved in stillness, and in eternity stood still, gazing at the One. And sure, I have observed here in this absence of a head capacity enough and more for the universe to flower in. But do I have room enough for another person? Can this way teach my heart to love and be compassionate and kind?

Why, after such dedication, do these qualities find so little space in me to grow as I hike this hard journey so straight down the empirical path to zero?

Cold and Heat 6

In the desert, without rain, the leaves and roots shrivel until one day I wake and see that the plant is gone. I search but find nowhere its shade, its companionship, its promise of flower and fruit. Only I feel the sand painful with heat as I sift it through my fingers, looking.

I sit on a rock. My fears rise before me like a mirage of a city full of shadowy people. I do not exist. Like the plant I have vanished into the sand as if I had never been. So many thoughts and emotions, so many dreams and hopes and intentions, so many relationships, come to nothing. To worse than nothing—to an awareness of nothing that deepens the nothingness.

Despair enters my heart. No, I cannot put it that way. I cannot say it enters my heart, for, like the plant, that organ has disappeared with the creeping exfoliation of my edges—all decayed, all disintegrated into nothingness. Like my breath, rising and falling in emptiness, the sinking feeling sinks only in the void. I am a nobody, a vacancy, a cipher—bodiless, mindless, heartless. I am the living dead.

What can I do? I came to live in the desert, and it has destroyed me. It is far too late now to lie down and die.

Cold and Heat 7

And so the path, for what it's worth, ends where it began, in the desert. No garlands decorate the finish line. No friends cheering, no honor or respectful looks. Only the absence of my self here to greet me.

All right. So let me greet myself. Let me say to myself, "Thus far have we come, dear heart, to emptiness. Let this be enough. Rest now. If the sun will burn, it will burn, but it will not burn what is already burnt away. If the cold will squeeze, let it squeeze, but it will not squeeze in its vise what is already too small to see. We have arrived at nothingness, and nothing now can hurt us anymore.

"And yet, heart, strangely, we live. Let me kiss you in this moment, and hold your hand, and stroll with you across the trackless waste, not searching, but softly wondering who, who, who we could possibly be."

VII

A Flower

Flower 1

In the early morning, I sit before my computer, waiting for words. The empty screen glows in the dark. I am afraid. What if, this time, no words come?

The fear prompts me to look back once again into the emptiness. Here is the primal blank, the utter bareness of the desert where no words dwell and yet out of which all these words come. I am at the mercy of this blank. Like someone at prayer who has come to the end of his own resources, I bow down before it and ask it for its words. And then in silence I wait for it to speak.

I have a theory about the blank. The blank stays so blank, so unknown to me, so unrevealing of its nature because it is not actually me. It is, rather, beyond me, an infinite and secret being holed up on the other side of my awareness. And so I call it 'the other.' Writing, I listen to this other. I take dictation, like a secretary, watching the words rise out of the blank like a child watching a magician pull rabbits from a hat. I have no knowledge of what words will appear, for the other is unknowable. It spills words out of itself like a cloudless sky dropping rain.

When I acknowledge this other as the source of my words, a change comes over me. My anxiety dissipates. I see the blank not as a threat but as my friend, and I turn to it with anticipation, surrendering to its mystery. What stories, I wonder, will it dream for me today? Upon what journey will it take me? And so I listen, and follow hints, and images, and intuitions. I am like an empty boat, venturing out on a strange and murky sea to fish for words. I cast my line into the blank and wait. And as the blank puts words into awareness, my fingers feed them into the computer where they rise a second time from the blank and take shape upon the screen.

If this theory about the other is true, then something else, also strange, is true: that this figuring out I am doing is not me but the blank floating ideas about itself. And it is this other, this absent one about whom I know nothing, who is the author of this book.

Flower 2

I leave my office to go to class, books and papers under my arm. The hallway, full of students, flows into this openness like a river flowing into the sea. I step into the crowded elevator. The door closes on one floor and opens on another, yet the elevator never moves, a miracle that seems to go unnoticed. I step out, and another hallway flows from the inexhaustible source, bringing on its current more students, a professor or two, a twisting corner, and finally a door. Creating an arm out of the nothing, I open the door and watch with interest the frame expand gracefully, stretching like an elastic band until its edges have vanished into this edgelessness. I am erased in this erasure, and in my absence find at once the classroom, the horseshoe of tables, and the students waiting for class to begin.

I greet the students, put a rough agenda on the board, and ask them to write for ten minutes in their journals, recording whatever thoughts arise. I sit at my desk and write also, the words appearing mysteriously out of the minute space between the pen tip and the paper. How every bit of the universe is a seed, incessantly sprouting and leafing.

After a few minutes, I pause and look out from this creative absence. Who is here in the room? I count fifteen students in the half circle but no teacher at my desk. The students are attending a teacherless class. And so my usual question about what *I* should do next disintegrates. The class is not centered on me, for I am absent. The class is centered on the students. What, therefore, I ask, should the *students* be doing to learn what they need to learn? And like a poet beseeching the Muse, I wait for the answer to arise out of my absence, out of that inscrutable teacher at the heart of the class.

At thirty, I embarked with misgivings on a teaching career. But I see now with relief that I never, ever, ever became a teacher.

Flower 3

I walk into the desert, not knowing what I will find. The sand blows across my feet. I have been here before, into this blankness, and yet it is not the same. Something is unfamiliar.

Beyond the hills, I hear again the rumble of thunder. The sound echoes within the mysterious vastness of the desert, within me and without me. Who is speaking here?

Kneeling down on the floor of the desert, I examine the sand. It is gold dust and silver. It is soil and seeds. It is only rock. In the end, I cannot tell what it is. I can only guess and move on.

I am looking for a flower and find none.

Across the desert, I see a column of dust moving in my direction. As it approaches, the outline of a figure appears at its core, shimmering like a mirage. I cannot believe what I see: my friend, walking towards me out of the secret depths of the desert. As he comes near, his eyes glint in the sun. Where has he come from? Where is he going?

We greet each other, and hug, and smile. How amazing, I say, meeting you here. He looks at me, and smiles again, and lifts his hand, pointing over my shoulder.

I guess his intention and speak first. "Want to go on a trip?" I say, grinning.

"OK," he replies. "Where to?"

"To smell the roses," I say.

"Ah, yes," he says, looking up and taking a deep breath, "the scent is everywhere."

Flower 4

I look out. I look in. Who is this "I" that looks?

When I look out and also look at who is looking out, I see no face, no person, no observer. Only clarity and light. No-one is here looking at the world. And yet the world before me is an observed world. Across its surface plays the sense that things are being looked at, as if a thin but infinite film of awareness is glued over all the scene. This awareness of the world carries within it also that awareness of the absence of a looker. In this odd but clear experience of absence combined with awakeness, I discover that I am.

I turn my attention from the world and look into the desert, into the place where nothing is. I gaze into absence, into nothingness, into utter emptiness. Here is neither clarity nor light nor even looking, but the absolute, unknowable darkness of non-existence. Here is no being or awareness at all. Yet over the surface of this impenetrable unawareness plays like a light the sense that it is an unawareness which is aware of being unaware—a strange kind of unawareness. And against the unclear edge of this unconsciousness, I am conscious that I am.

I look out, and I look in. I know myself as pure awareness, a layer of looking with the world on one side and non-existence on the other. Like the surface of a calm lake, I display in this awareness the images of my life and join them to the unfathomable depths of non-being below. Between the two—between the world and non-being—I am aware that I am aware.

Where does this awareness come from? Not from the world, which comes and goes within the unchanging wakefulness. From non-existence then? Out of darkness, out of nothingness, without roots, do I rise like a magical flower into the light of myself?

Flower 5

On the rough days, I get that sinking feeling. Or the resentment and the anger rise in me. Or guilt. No matter who I think or see I am, negative feelings still come strongly, hurting.

What can I do? I can only stand in the desert and look at them—and appreciate the fact that, like my physical sensations, the feelings do not come and go within any edges. The sadness is not, in truth, in my heart, for in the desert I find no heart—only sensations intertwining with feelings in the emptiness. Uncontained, my sadness and my anger and my guilt express themselves in edgeless space, in the sensitive but invulnerable heart of the One.

When I observe my feelings floating thus in awareness, I see that in the freedom that surrounds them, I am free. Angry, I am free of anger, for here is no person who is angry. No strings attach the anger to me, for here is no me to which anything can attach. And yet this freedom is not uncaring. It holds within its infinite and feather-light embrace the anger, and listens to it, and looks at it with gentle eyes. It is as if the anger were a fierce and ugly monster, roaring in the wild, which slowly, under the unconditional and loving gaze of the One, quietens, and transforms, like a child removing a Halloween disguise, and becomes instead of anger something else. What stories in the safety of the One it soon feels safe to tell, of hurts—not my hurts but its own, for I am not—and what deep breaths of freedom do I draw, listening to it speak.

Sometimes, not often, but when the listening persists and seems to make room in its infinitude for the deepest places, the feeling, whatever it has become, drops stories, drops names and language, drops all definition, and in the emptiness, naked, like a river running wild over rocks, reveals itself to be at heart the intimate, unknowable energy of the One.

Flower 6

High in the Sierras, I sit by a lake and watch my six-year-old daughter, Simone, laughing and splashing in the water with a friend. The sun flashes on her face, glancing off her eyes and teeth with bright pleasure. How free and happy she is, I think, and I smile.

Who is smiling?

I find here no me, no face or personality, to smile. Only I find the desert, impersonal, unmoved, the same emptiness I have always witnessed in this place.

And yet I am smiling at my daughter.

I touch my mouth, curious, my hand seeming to approach the transparency of a camera lens, not a head. I could be anyone and no-one. Fingertips disappear into the emptiness, sensations arise in the emptiness—the texture of a mouth without a mouth, the curve of a smile without a person smiling.

Who, then, is smiling?

Who else, I realize, but the desert itself. Without eyes or mouth or heart or brain, it—I—thinks and feels and speaks and sees. Naked, it is clothed in the scene at the lake and the response to that scene: *my* daughter playing in the water, *my* smile beaming across the sky, the deeply personal blossoming in the absolute impersonality of the void.

Later, long after the trip, tired and grouchy and feeling old, I pause in the rush of life and ask myself, Who struggles thus? Whose limbs want rest? Whose heart sinks in the face of yet another challenge? And again I find here no human being in the way, blameable in his imperfection for the limitations of my life. It is, instead, this impersonal One who, eternally perfect and free, desires in this moment more than anything else to cry, to sleep, to run away into freedom and be free.

And so, by a long, roundabout route, I have returned to my childhood, to find the one who was lost on the moor, and the one who in all my later years of wandering was lost. It was not a boy or a boy-within-a-man who was alone and feared, who cried or could not cry, not someone who, in this vision of the desert, must disappear or be transcended. In all the difficulties and intractable places, as well as in the joys, it has been this One, this emptiness, this impersonal and unchanging void who has seen, and felt, and grown, and come slowly to accept, indeed to love, the very human life it lives.

Flower 7

In the night, I wake and feel the weight of the coming day. Problems and tasks crowd to the side of my bed, stretching out in a wide, dense circle well beyond the day's next evening, beyond many days' evenings, beyond my sense of ever being able to handle them. Their number and their gravity overwhelm me. They are too many and too much.

Under this pressure, I see, finally, at long last, after so many attempts to find solutions, to handle everything, to come out right in the end, that I am not able to do so. My problems are greater than my capacity to deal with them. Endless, they seem to thrive on my retreat, keep coming, strengthen, multiply, make more and more demands on me until I am, as I am now, thoroughly and deeply beaten by their affront.

And so for what feels like the first time in my life, I find no alternative but to hand the whole vast set of difficulties which have defeated me over—to what? To what is apparently suddenly waiting to receive them, that mysterious resource deeper than myself, that unknown other, that being in the desert. At the edge of my own capacity, alone, stumbling, more than stumbling, kneeling in failure and submission, I discover in surprise that the One is holding out its hand to take—in fact, has already taken into its love—the impasse of my life.

I look around. How strange. The crowd of problems I confronted when I woke has dispersed, as if it were all imaginary. The light grows outside, filtering through the blinds. I get out of bed, begin the day. Unaccountably, I have more time than before. Each problem that comes to me comes singly, is limited, its solution arising easily not out of me but out of the One that underlies and is present with me. The future and its endless line of difficulties have dissolved into this simple intimacy, into this knowledge that when the problems that will come do in their turn come into the space, the space is big enough and wise enough to deal with them—in an odd sense has already dealt with them.

It is perhaps only a feeling, this sense of trust, a precious but passing flower in the vast eternity of the desert. But in its presence, my heart bows down and worships and sings to the One an endless hymn of gratitude and praise.

Flower 8

Rain is falling in the night. I peek through the blinds and see water flowing steadily down the gutters in the street. It will be good for the earth, good for the plants, I think, and I go back to bed.

I lie there invisible, listening to the sound of the rain as it shifts in intensity and mixes with the sound of the gusting wind. It mixes also, I notice, with the sound of my breathing and of Carol's breathing, coming and going together in emptiness. Whose sounds are these? I wonder. Who is breathing, without nose or lungs? Who listens without ears? And who lies here awake in the ever-awake, trying to fall asleep?

In the morning, the sun streams through the gaps in the blinds. I lie in bed watching fragmentary feelings and images play briefly in the light and disappear, like drifting motes of dust. A heavy feeling, a depression, comes suddenly, like a large black spider descending out of nowhere. I watch it closely for a while, observing with relief that it finds no nook in me in which to hide and build its web. Instead, it hovers in the awakeness, like a cloud in a clear sky, singing its hopelessness to me.

Carol stirs and smiles, and I smile back. Simone in her room makes no sound. I get up, and brew tea, and look into awareness. How reliable it is, how always present, how simple and profound. Like an archer whose only task is to shoot at the target, I aim only at the desert. But as the arrow pierces the emptiness, it roots, and sprouts, and puts forth leaves, and flowers into this ordinary, extraordinary world.

VIII

Seasons

Seasons 1

I have lived many years in the desert. I have seen the sun rise and set a myriad times over its rim, bringing the heat and the light and leaving behind it a void filled by the cold and the beautiful stars. I have seen rain, too, and mirages, and leaves and flowers like magic pushing their way out of the sand—for a day, a month, a year, but always in the end dying back into the desert. Observing these changes, I have begun to see how stable is the desert, how always I can find in it a place to stand, or walk, or lie, whatever the weather or the season.

Sometimes I try to remember when it was that I first came into the desert, but I cannot trust my memory. I recall the room in the country house, and Douglas, and the pointing, and my brother next to me, and I tell myself that that was the beginning. But then I see around the edges of the image the emptiness again. And the image and the series of images that follow and form the story of my life appear to me as but more flowers, growing and blooming for a moment in the desert, and then returning into the eternal emptiness.

And so I begin to think that my arrival in the desert was only a myth dreamed while I was sleeping and that, in fact, I have never lived anywhere else.

Sleeping? Another myth, for in this place no eye ever shut, nor opened to behold the always-awake.

Desert? A useful image, but one which will, with all the rest and all these words, die into emptiness.

In the end, what am I left with? I am left with nothing but the simple experience. And so, once again, I raise my finger, and point, and look, and find with surprise that the bareness itself is the most beautiful flower of all.

Seasons 2

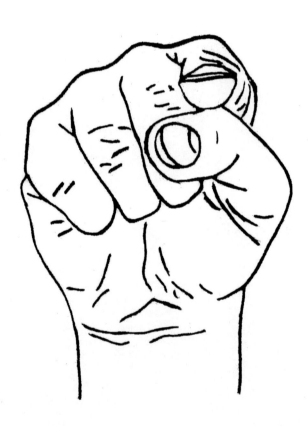

Appendix A: Experiments

The experiences I have described in the main part of this book grow out of the spiritual path originated by Douglas Harding. One of the key principles of this path is that seeing your own absence/presence, or Who you really are, is easy. All you have to do is look in the right place. Harding's special contribution in this respect is what he calls "experiments," which, if performed honestly, make it impossible for you to miss the experience of your real self.

In several sections of this book, I have described my experiences with some of these experiments. However, the most important thing for you, of course, is not my experience but your own. Beyond reading about this way, you should take the opportunity, I suggest, if you haven't already, of *experiencing* it for yourself. In order to make this easy for you, I have included here directions for conducting five experiments. If you follow the directions carefully, you should have no difficulty in seeing Who you really are.

General Directions:

First, pay attention to what you experience with your senses and ignore, for the duration of the experiments, what you imagine, believe, or remember. In other words, take a fresh look. Second, if you discover something different from what is implied or stated as a likely finding in an experiment, honor your own experience and reject what you have read.

1. The Pointing Experiment

The pointing experiment is a basic one. It asks you to pay attention to and acknowledge what you see instead of overlooking or ignoring what you see.

First, point your index finger at an object in front of you. Notice that your finger is an object with a shape, edge, and color and that the object you are pointing at also has shape, edges, and color.

Next, point at one of your feet. Notice again that your finger and your foot both have shape, edges, and color. In other words, a thing is pointing at a thing.

Now point at your belly. Isn't it the same situation again? Isn't your finger—an object with shape, edges, and color—pointing at another thing which has shape, edges, and color?

Finally, point at your face. Is that what you are actually doing? Is your finger, which has shape, edges, and color, pointing at a face which, in your present experience, has shape, edges, and color? Is your finger right now pointing at any thing at all? Isn't it rather pointing at the absence of your face, at your "no-face," at what is like a clear window with no edges or color or shape at all?

2. The Touching Experiment

This is a useful experiment for exploring the question of whether the sight of your absence or "no-face" is contradicted by the physical sensation of touching your face.

Point again at your no-face. Notice again that your finger is pointing at no thing, that it is pointing not at a surface but at clear openness.

Now bring your finger forward and touch your forehead. You will see that the tip of your finger has disappeared into the openness, into the no-face. You will also notice that you get a "spot" of physical sensation. Pay close attention to that sensation, please, and at the same time observe your no-face. Does the openness of the no-face disappear when you feel the physical sensation? Or, to put it another way, do you *see* your face attached to the spot of physical sensation? Is the physical sensation inside or on a face, a head, or anything at all? Isn't the physical sensation simply happening in the open space of the no-face?

Move your finger around your face. Different sensations will arise, different textures and warmths. But isn't the basic situation the same: sensations coming and going in the no-face rather than your face?

What about your nose, that shape that sticks out of your no-face? Isn't it just like your finger, disappearing into the openness at its near end? Sure, you can see a bit of it there, rather fuzzy probably, but what is it attached to? Is the rest of your face your side of it? Or isn't your edgeless, colorless, shapeless no-face your side of that nose?

3. *The Turning Experiment*

The question here is, Do you move?

First, please stand up. Point your finger again at your no-face, and notice again that your finger is not pointing at a thing but instead is pointing at no thing or clarity.

Now, very slowly, turn around (and continue turning around), still looking at your finger pointing at your no-face. You will see that beyond or behind your finger, the background moves. For example, if you are in a room, slightly blurred walls and the door slide past beyond your finger. But notice also that, when you look at what your finger is pointing at, nothing there (or, rather, here) goes by. Nothing here moves. Nothing here is blurred, because nothing is here to move or to blur. So, let me ask you this: What is really moving here? You—or the world?

4. The Friend Experiment

You've looked a lot at your finger. Let's substitute your friend's face for your finger and at the same time still ask you to notice your clear and open no-face.

Look at your friend's face. Or if your friend is not around, look at your own face in a mirror.

Notice that the face you are looking at has two eyes. Does your no-face have two eyes, or any eyes at all? Notice that the face you are looking at has a mouth. Does your no-face have a mouth? Notice that the face you are looking at has an edge around it. Does your no-face have an edge around it? Isn't it edgeless or boundless? Notice that the face you are looking at has color and texture. Does your no-face have color or texture, or isn't it clear? Notice, finally, that the face you are looking at has a surface. Is there any surface where you are? Aren't you a clear openness in which is displayed now the face you are looking at?

5. *The Thought Experiment*

This is the last experiment. It's an interesting and relevant experiment if you are curious about how your mind fits in with your no-face.

I'm going to ask you to think of three words beginning with a specific letter. I'll give you the letter in a moment. As you think of the words, primarily notice where they come from. Do they pop up inside a head? Do they pop up inside a mind? Or don't they simply pop up out of nowhere?

OK. Here is the letter. Think of three words beginning with the letter "b."

Isn't it odd? Can you say where the words come from or where they are displayed? We conventionally say that our thoughts are in our minds. But in this experiment, did you experience your own, personal mind—*mind* in the sense of a separate place where your thoughts popped up? Can you find any edges to the place where your thoughts are displayed? Try the experiment again with a new letter, the letter "t," and look again for the container of your thoughts. Is there one?

Well, those are the five experiments. I hope that you have tried them and not just read about them, for probably the best way to answer the question, Who am I? is simply to look.

Appendix B: Resources

The most complete resource available is a website: www.headless.org. Here you can find an explanation of the philosophy of Douglas Harding and the 'headless way,' descriptions and mini-films of experiments you can perform on your own or with friends, the opportunity to buy related books and dvds, access to an email newsletter and a live discussion forum, and a schedule of workshops on offer around the world.

CONSCIOUS.TV is a TV channel which broadcasts on the Internet at www.conscious.tv. It also has programmes shown on several satellite and cable channels round the world including the Sky system in the UK where you can watch programmes at 9pm every evening on channel No 275. The channel aims to stimulate debate, question, enquire, inform, enlighten, encourage and inspire people in the areas of Consciousness, Non-Duality and Science. It also has a section called 'Life Stories' with many fascinating interviews.

There are over 200 interviews to watch including several with communicators on Non-Duality including Jeff Foster, Steve Ford, Suzanne Foxton, Gangaji, Greg Goode, Scott Kiloby, Richard Lang, Francis Lucille, Roger Linden, Wayne Liquorman, Jac O'Keefe, Mooji, Catherine Noyce, Tony Parsons, Halina Pytlasinska, Genpo Roshi, Satyananda, Richard Sylvester, Rupert Spira, Florian Schlosser, Mandi Solk, James Swartz, and Pamela Wilson. There is also an interview with UK Krishnamurti. Some of these interviewees also have books available from Non-Duality Press.

Do check out the channel as we are interested in your feedback and any ideas you may have for future programmes. Email us at info@conscious.tv with your ideas or if you would like to be on our email newsletter list.

WWW.CONSCIOUS.TV

CONSCIOUS.TV and NON-DUALITY PRESS
present two unique DVD releases

CONVERSATIONS ON NON-DUALITY – VOLUME 1
Tony Parsons – The Open Secret • Rupert Spira –
The Transparency of Things – Parts 1 & 2 • Richard Lang –
Seeing Who You Really Are

CONVERSATIONS ON NON-DUALITY – VOLUME 2
Jeff Foster – Life Without a Centre • Richard Sylvester –
I Hope You Die Soon • Roger Linden – The Elusive Obvious

Available to order from: www.non-dualitypress.com

New Book now available to order from NON-DUALITY PRESS

CONVERSATIONS ON NON-DUALITY
Twenty-Six Awakenings

The book explores the nature of true happiness, awakening, enlightenment and the 'Self' to be realised. It features 26 expressions of liberation, each shaped by different life experiences and offering a unique perspective.

The collection explores the different ways 'liberation' happened and 'suffering' ended. Some started with therapy, self-help workshops or read books written by spiritual masters, while others travelled to exotic places and studied with gurus. Others leapt from the despair of addiction to drugs and alcohol to simply waking up unexpectedly to a new reality.

The 26 interviews included in the book are with: David Bingham, Daniel Brown, Sundance Burke, Katie Davis, Peter Fenner, Steve Ford, Jeff Foster, Suzanne Foxton, Gagaji, Richard Lang, Roger Linden, Wayne Liquorman, Francis Lucille, Mooji, Catherine Noyce, Jac O'Keeffe, Tony Parsons, Bernie Prior, Halina Pytlasinska, Genpo Roshi, Florian Schlosser, Mandi Solk, Rupert Spira, James Swartz, Richard Sylvester and Pamela Wilson.

Lightning Source UK Ltd.
Milton Keynes UK
UKOW02f1441071114

241271UK00001B/18/P